iPhone 15 Camera Mastery Guide

Illustrated for Beginners, Seniors, & Content
Creators to Use the Pro and Max Series Cam:
Hidden Modes, Settings, Tips & Tricks in iOS
17 For Photography & Videography

Jack E. Brandon

D1248363

Table of content

INTRODUCTION

Apple always adds new features to the camera system in new iPhones, and the iPhone 15 series is no different. According to MacRumors, they have a lot of information about the cameras in the iPhone 15 line, from the regular iPhone 15 with its upgraded 48-megapixel camera to the iPhone 15 Pro Max with its new periscope telephoto lens.

iPhone 15 and 15 Plus

The 48MP main camera is the most important new thing about the iPhone 15 and iPhone 15 Plus. The camera should take pictures that are brighter, more colorful, and with more detail than the iPhone 14 since it has a wider aperture and a higher default resolution of 24MP. The iPhone 15 probably won't use the Sony IMX-803 image sensor that was in the iPhone 14 Pro. Instead, it will use a different Sony sensor that is better at what it does.

Because it has more pixels, you can zoom in on photos up to two times without losing quality, which happens on phones that don't have telephoto cameras.

The ultrawide camera and selfie camera are still the same 12MP units from the iPhone 14 line. But Apple said that the whole camera system would take better pictures in low light and with HDR color, so these should still work better than older iPhones.

Portrait mode has also been changed. The Camera app will now use Portrait mode instantly if it sees a good subject, just like older iPhones did with macro or night modes. When you take a picture, you don't have to use portrait mode. You can turn it on later in the Photos app, or you can change the focus to make the picture look different if you didn't get it right the first time.

iPhone 15 Pro and iPhone 15 Pro Max

The 48MP main camera from the iPhone 14 Pro is in the iPhone 15 Pro and iPhone 15 Pro Max. It has a different sensor than the one in the iPhone 15 and 15 Plus. It can shoot in both 24MP and 48MP and in either ProRAW or HEIF. The iPhone 14 Pro had to use ProRAW to make the most of all its pixels, so it's good that Apple has now added a compact format for people who want to save on storage space.

Apple says that the main camera's usual mode is like a 24mm lens, which is good for taking pictures with a lot of depth. You can set a 28mm or 35mm equivalent, which lets you focus on a specific topic, if you'd rather have your camera zoomed in more by default, for example for taking portraits.

The two Pros have different telephoto cameras. The camera on the iPhone 15 Pro has 12MP and a 3x optical zoom. The camera on the iPhone 15 Pro Max has the same 12MP sensor but a 5x optical zoom.

The ultrawide camera and selfie camera on the Pro models are the same as they were on the iPhone 15 and 15 Plus. However, Apple has made software changes that make them better.

The iPhone 15 Pro models can now shoot up to 4K ProRes video at 60 frames per second, and they can record this directly to an external drive that is attached to the iPhone 15 Pro's USB-C port. This makes it easier to capture large video files without filling up your iPhone's storage. The method used to set video color while editing is also available for people who are good at what they do.

CHAPTER 1

Camera Basics

Open Camera

You can swipe left from the lock screen or tap the Camera button on the home screen to open the camera on your iPhone.

For your safety, a green dot shows up in the top right corner of the screen when the camera is on.

Take a picture or Video

- Press either the volume up or down button or the camera button to take a picture.

Tip: To take a QuickTake video, touch and hold the shutter button while the camera is in Photo mode.

Change the camera's modes

The camera is already in photo mode when you turn it on for the first time. Use the Photo mode to take shots that are both still and moving. Swipe the screen left or right to choose one of these camera options:

- **Videos**: Record videos.

- **Time-Lapse:** Make a video that shows how things change over time.

- **Slo-mo:** Make a movie that looks like it was shot in slow motion.

- **Pano:** Take a picture of a scene or a moment in time as a whole.

- **Portrait**: Use depth-of-field to make your picture look better.

- **Cinematic:** Use the depth-of-field effect to make your videos look more like movies.

- **Square:** The square aspect ratio is what you should use when taking pictures.

There are three different aspect ratios for the iPhone 15, Pro, and Pro Max. To switch between square, 4:3, and 16:9 aspect ratios, press the Camera Controls button and then press 4:3.

Zoom in or out

On the iPhone 15 Pro and iPhone 15 Pro Max, there are four levels of optical-quality zoom. There are four different levels of zoom: **5X** uses an ultra-wide lens, **1X** uses a primary wide lens, **2X** also uses a primary lens, and **3X** uses a telephoto lens.

The idea is that Apple can get a 2X zoom without losing quality by using the 12MP sensor in the middle of the 48MP sensor. To be very technical, there is some quality loss because Apple can't use pixel binning at this time. This means that the smaller pixels gather a little less light.

Still, the shots will be better than when you use digital zoom. Digital zoom doesn't change the optics; instead, it crops the picture, which makes the image less clear.

These zoom settings are already set, and you can change them by tapping the circles above the shutter button. When you tap on any of them, there is a little-known trick that allows you to hold and slide your finger up or down.

There will be a zoom wheel that you can use to change the amount of zoom up to 15X. The focal length that goes with each zoom setting is shown below them.

When you're done, you can either let it go away on its own or spin the wheel in the direction of the shutter to get rid of it. The other option is to pinch in or out, but it is less useful and blocks the screen.

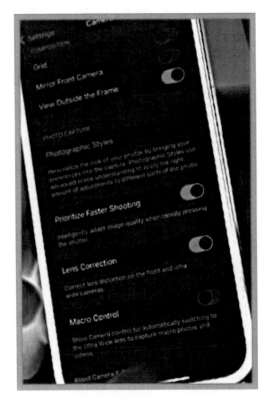

To use Macro Mode on your phone, bring it very close to the thing you want to photograph. It can focus a few millimeters away from the lens. There is a switch in Settings that you can flip to stop this from happening automatically.

Quick Start Guide

Icon to Know

To begin, you should know that symbols are yellow when they are on and white when they are off.

Flash: You can turn the flash on or off or set it to auto mode. If there isn't enough light in the shot, auto mode will turn on the flash. The iPhone's flash is made to make the exact color temperature of white light you need for the scene you're shooting. It works well and is a great piece of engineering.

HDR: This stands for "**High Dynamic Range**." The goal is to get better results when taking pictures of places with a lot of shade or a lot of light.

The camera takes 3 pictures when you take a HDR picture:

- A picture with a standard exposure.

- A picture that is overexposed but allows for good dark detail.
- An underexposed image, which means that the brightness is lowered so that white parts don't bloom and show detail.

Live Photo: Live Photo takes a picture and records video for 1.5 seconds before and after the picture is taken. This makes a picture move when you tap or press on the iPhone screen.

Timer: Set the timer to 3 or 10 seconds, and then run like crazy to get in the shot. The 3-second setting is for Olympians, and the 10-second setting is for drunk or intoxicated people.

Camera Rotate: This lets you switch between seeing what's in front of and behind the camera. The camera on the front of the phone always takes better photos and movies, but the camera on the back is great for taking selfies.

Video: It was shot in 16:9, which is the same aspect ratio as a widescreen TV. You can change the video settings in the iPhone's settings, which are explained below.

Slo-Mo: While you're recording regular video, you can move in and out of Slo-Mo. You can change the Slo-Mo options in the iPhone options, which are explained below.

Time-Lapse: Your iPhone takes shots at set times. The action looks much faster when played at normal speed. The iPhone decides how long to wait between shots based on how long the recording lasts. This can't be changed, so just enjoy the effects.

SE	SLO-MO	VIDEO	PHOTO	SQUARE	PANO

Photos Library: This button takes you right to the iPhone's Photos Library.

Shutter Button: To take a picture, press the shutter button once in Photo mode. Hold down the camera button to take a bunch of pictures at once. It's great for getting a picture of something moving quickly. It's very simple to shoot bursts by chance. Don't worry, you can get rid of them later.

Filters: This is only shown in Photo and Square mode. There are 8 effects you can use when you tap the icon: Mono, Tonal, Noir, Fade, Chrome, Process, Transfer, and Instant.

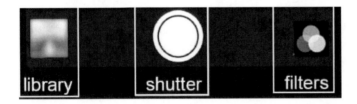

CHAPTER 2

Camera Tools

Adjusting Focus and Exposure

Before taking a picture, the iPhone 15 camera instantly changes the focus, exposure, and face detection to make sure that the exposure is the same on all faces. To change the camera's exposure and focus by hand, do these things:

- Open the Camera app.
- Click on the screen to see the brightness setting and the area that will be focused automatically.
- Press on the spot where you want to change the focus.
  - If you want to change the exposure, move the Adjust Exposure button next to the focus area up or down.

When you find AE/AF Lock, touch and hold down the focus area until you see it. Then, press the screen to open the settings.

On the iPhone 15, Pro, and Pro models, you can control and lock the exposure for upcoming photos. When you press the Camera Controls and Exposure buttons, drag the exposure slider. There is no way to change the exposure until the camera is opened again. Go to Settings > Camera > Preserve Settings and turn on Exposure Adjustment. This will save the exposure control so that it doesn't get changed every time you open the camera.

Turn camera flash on or off

The flash on your iPhone camera is set to turn on by itself when it's needed. Follow these steps to control the flash by hand before taking a picture:

- To turn on or off the automatic flash on the iPhone 15, Pro, and Pro Max, press and hold the Flash button.
- Press the Camera Controls icon and then tap the flash button below the frame to set the flash to Auto, On, or Off.

Take a photo with a filter

- Open the camera app.
- The next step is to pick the Photo or Portrait mode.
  - After that, tap the Camera Controls icon before clicking the Filters icon.

- Swipe left or right on the filters below the viewer to see what they look like. Press on one to use it.

In Photos, you can change or get rid of a photo's filter.

Use a timer

You can set the timer on your iPhone's camera to give yourself enough time to get ready for the shot.

To set a timer;

- Open the camera.
- Next, on your iPhone 15, Pro, or Pro Max, press the Camera Controls button, then press the Timer button and pick 3s or 10s.
- Finally, press the Shutter button to begin the timer.

Align your photo using a grid

- To show a grid on the camera screen, go to Settings > Camera and turn on the Grid feature. With this, you can line up and plan your shots better.

After taking a picture, you can use the Photos app's editing tools to better align the shots and change the horizontal and vertical viewpoints.

CHAPTER 3

Photographic Styles
What is a photographic style?

A feature of the iOS camera called Photographic Styles allows you to select from several settings that change the color, brightness, contrast, and vibrancy of the image. You can then use a slider to change these settings to fit your chosen style of photography. This way, you won't have to edit or add a filter after the fact.

However, you can't take away the settings like you can with a filter after the shot is taken.

Once you choose a Photographic Style, every time you take a picture in Photo mode, your phone's camera will use those settings. You can still change them in the camera itself, though.

Picking a Photographic style
The camera takes an accurate and fair stance because it is set to standard by default. Add your unique picture style by doing the following:

- Once the Camera app is open, press the **Camera Controls button**.

- Press the **"Photographic Styles" button** and then swipe to the left to see a sample of the different styles.

1. **Rich Contrast:** It creates a striking effect when the shadows are darker, the colors are brighter, and the contrast is higher.
2. **Vibrant:** Colors that are bright and vivid look very realistic.
3. **Warm:** Undertones of gold make things seem warmer.
4. **Cool:** When you look at something with blue colors, it seems cooler.

To change the style of the picture, press the Tone and Warmth buttons below the frame. To change the value, slide the slider to the left or right. For a fresh start, press the "Reset" button next to Photographic Styles.

- To use a photographic style, tap the **Photographic Styles button**.
- If you want to change a photographic style, click the **"Photographic Styles On"** button at the top of the screen.

You can change Photographic Styles in Settings by going to **Options** > **Camera** > **Photographic Styles**.

change photographic styles from settings

1. On your iPhone, open the Settings app.

2. Scroll up and click on Camera.

3. Pick out photographic styles.

4. You can swipe between the Standard (the default) style, Rich Contrast, Vibrant, Warm, and Cool styles.

5. Select *Use "Style"* on the one you want.

CHAPTER 4

How To Use Camera Modes

Take a live photo with your iPhone camera

Apple's Live Photos are a mix of photos and videos that record what happens 1.5 seconds before and after you press the snap button. You can play Live Photos, which combines pictures, music, and movement, with just a touch and hold. It's not enough to just take a pretty picture with Live Photos; you can record the whole scene, including sound and movement, in the same easy way you would take any other picture.

You might not need or want to see motion or hear music, or you might want to get rid of the extra room that these hybrid pictures take up. That being said, there are ways to make Live Photos smaller and even turn existing ones into regular photos. People often forget to turn off Live Photos, even though it's very easy to do so. This means that every picture you take is live and takes up twice as much space on your phone.

When you open the Camera app, the Live Photos moving yellow bullseye icon will show up in the upper right corner of your screen. There will also be an arrow icon in the upper center that lets you change the camera settings. If you tap the bullseye, it will turn off, and you'll see a short message telling you so. If you cut through a white bullseye button on top, the function stops working. To turn off Live Photos until you want them to be on again, go to Settings > Camera > Preserve Settings and turn off Live Photos until you want it on.

After you turn off Live Photos, any pictures you take will be regular stills. However, any Live Photos you already took will still be Live Photos in your Camera Roll. The middle top arrow in the Camera app can also be used to change how Live Photos are set up. This gives you a lot of power over things like Live Photos, flash, video, lighting, aspect ratio, timer, and more. One-touch changes let you choose between Live Off, Live On, and Auto while you're out and about.

Friends and family can receive Live Photos, but they will only move if they have an iPhone, iPad, or iPod Touch. Here's what you need to do to turn a Live Photo into a still picture: Open the Live Photo and select Edit. Make any changes you need to, like cropping, and then hit the bullseye icon to pick a frame.

How to take a Live Photo

You can take Live Photos with your iPhone's camera. A Live Shot catches the sound from the few seconds before and after the picture is taken. Taking a picture is the same as taking a live picture.

- First, make sure the camera is on.
- Make sure the camera is in photo mode and Live Photo is turned on.

When Live Photo is on, the button for Live Photo can be seen at the top of the screen. There is a straight line through the Live Photo button, which means that the feature is not on. Tap the button to turn Live Photo on or off.

- To take a live picture, press the camera button.
- Select the picture thumbnail at the bottom of the screen and then tap and hold the screen to play the live photo.

How can I get access to my live photos on any of the iPhone 15 models?

1. Start up the Photos app.
2. Click on Albums.

3. Use the drop-down menu to choose Live Photos as the type of media.

4. Pick out any picture you want.

5. To play the Live Photo, tap and hold the screen.

Editing live pictures

Here's how to change live photos on any model of the iPhone 15:

1. Open the Photos app and go to the Photos section.

1. Pick out the Live Photo that you want to change.

2. Select Edit and keep making the changes you've already made.

3. Press "Done" when you're done.

How to use depth control

Now you can use depth control on any iPhone 15 by following these steps:

Step 1: Pick a picture in portrait mode to work on with Depth Control.

Step 2: choose Edit from the drop-down menu. Next, choose Depth Control. An icon would show up at the bottom of the screen.

Step 3: Move the tool to the left or right side of the screen to change the intensity of the picture.

Step 4: Press "Done" when you're done.

Capture action shots with iPhone camera burst mode

An iPhone camera app feature called Burst mode, also known as Continuous Shooting Mode, allows users to take multiple photos at once.

When you press and hold the camera button on an iPhone 15 model, it no longer turns on burst mode. Instead, it turns on QuickTake.

Find out a new way to use Burst mode here.

1. Press and hold the shutter button for portrait shots, then move it to the left side of the screen right away.
2. For landscape pictures, press down on the shutter button and quickly move it up.
3. Take your finger off the screen when you're done shooting.

Let's Take a Selfie

1. On your iPhone, open the Camera app 📷.

2. Tap ⟳ to go to the camera on the front of the phone.

3. Put your iPhone in front of you.

Tip: To make the field of view bigger, tap the arrows inside the frame.

4. To take a picture or start recording, press the shutter button or the volume button.

Let's shoot a panorama

1. On your iPhone, open the Camera app .

2. Pick Pano mode.

3. Press the Shutter button.

4. Move slowly along the center line in the direction of the arrow.

5. Press the Shutter button one more time to finish.

If you want to look the other way, tap the arrow. Turn your iPhone to landscape mode to pan vertically. If you have a vertical pan, you can also turn it around.

CHAPTER 5

Other Cool Camera Mode

Macro Photos and Videos

The camera takes macro photos, which are amazing close-ups that are focused, with the Ultra Wide camera. You can take Live Photos and macro photos, as well as macro short-time movies and time-lapse videos.

Shoot Macro photos / Video

- Start up the Camera app.
- On your screen, right above the snap button, make sure that Photo is selected as the camera mode.
  - You can get as close to your subject as 2 cm (0.79 inches).

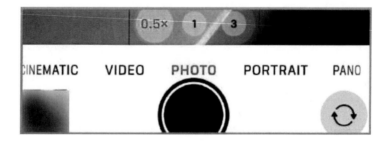

  - When you switch to close-up mode, you'll see a blurred or fuzzy picture.
  - Right now, switching between normal picture mode and macro mode is automatic. But Apple

wants to add a setting to change that in the future.

- Take your shots.
- Follow the same steps to make iPhone 15 macro videos.
- When you switch from regular video to macro video, it's not as clear as when you switch between pictures.
- The ultra-wide lens will auto-focus when taking macro photos and videos, but you can still touch the screen to change the focus and exposure by hand.

Shoot Macro video in slow motion or time lapse

1. Open your iPhone's camera app and choose either Slo-mo or Time-lapse mode.
1. Press the .5x button to switch to the Ultra Wide camera. Next, get close to the subject.
2. To start and stop recording, tap the Record button.

Automatic macro switching control

You can choose when the camera will automatically switch to the Ultra Wide camera so that you can take macro photos and videos.

1. Turn on your iPhone's camera and move in close to your subject.

When you're close enough to your subject, 🌸 shows up on the screen.

2. Tap 🌸 to stop macro changes automatically.

Tip: You can go back up or tap if the photo or video gets blurry .5x to move to the camera that sees in ultra wide.

3. Tap 🌸 it to turn on automatic swapping between macros again.

Go to Settings ⚙ > Camera and turn off Macro Control. This will stop the camera from automatically switching to the Ultra Wide camera for macro photos and movies.

Go to Settings 📷 > Camera > Preserve Settings and then turn on Macro Control. This will save your macro control setting between camera sessions.

Take a picture in portrait mode

When you want to take a picture, use the Camera app in either video, portrait, or photo mode.

- First things first, open the Camera.
- To switch to the front-facing camera, press the **Camera Chooser Back-Facing or Camera Chooser Back-Facing button.**
- The iPhone needs to be in front of you.

If you have an iPhone 15, you can make your view bigger by tapping the arrows inside the frame.

- To record or take a picture, press any of the sound buttons or the shutter button.

Go to Settings > Camera and turn on Mirror Front Camera or Mirror Front Photos to take a selfie that captures the image as it appears in the front-facing camera frame rather than backward.

Set depth control to portrait

Make changes to the amount of blur in the background of your photos with the Depth Control slider.

1. Open Camera ⬛ and choose Portrait mode, then frame your subject.

2. Press ⓕ in the screen's upper right corner.

The slider for the Depth Control shows up below the screen.

3. To change the effect, move the slider to the right or left.

4. Press the "Shutter" button to take the picture.

You can change how blurry the background is after taking a picture of a person using the Depth Control tool in the Photos app ❀.

Portrait Lightening Effects

You can pretty much change where and how bright the Portrait Lighting is to make eyes stand out or to brighten and smooth out face features.

1. Open Camera, select Portrait mode then drag ⬡ to pick a lighting effect.

2. Press ⬡ at the screen's top bar.

The slider for Portrait Lighting shows up below the frame.

3. To change the effect, move the slider to the right or left.

4. Press the "Shutter" button to take the picture.

Take a picture with Night Mode

Not all devices can take good pictures in night mode without having some kind of problem. But now that the new iPhone 15 models are out, iPhone photographers can use Night mode to take beautiful shots at any time of day.

To allow more light to enter and make your photo graphs appear brighter, night mode lengthens the exposure time. You don't have to choose between a regular picture and a Night mode picture on the iPhone; when it's dark, Night mode turns on and adjusts itself instantly.

How to utilize the iPhone's Night Mode

Night mode will automatically turn on whenever you try to take a photo in low light. The moon-shaped icon in the upper left corner will turn yellow. The exposure time will be shown by a time like "1s" or "5s" next to the moon sign when it is used.

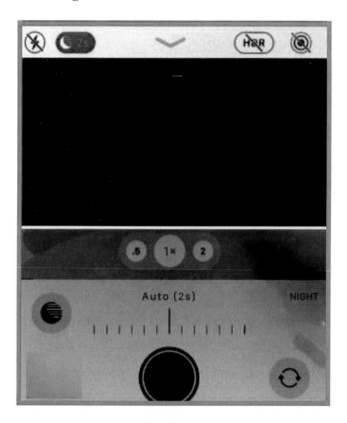

Again, press the round camera button to take a picture when Night mode is on. Hold the camera as still as possible until the exposure is over. This can be hard at first, but you need to allow the camera time to take in light to get a good night shot.

How can I change the time it takes to take a picture in Night mode?

There will be an exposure time next to the moon icon on your iPhone when Night mode is on. This tells you how long it will take to take a good Night mode photo. You can, however, change the timing by hand if you want a faster or better image.

1. In the camera app, tap the Night mode icon when it's dark and Night mode has been turned on for the suggested amount of time.

Quick note: The moon sign will show when it's not quite dark enough to turn on Night mode automatically, but it will be grayed out. You can still tap the sign to make it work or change it.

2. Sliders will show up below the frame. Move them to the right to add more light or to the left to remove light. Anyone who wants more light will only be able to choose "Max." This allows the camera to take as long as it needs to get the best possible Night mode shot. You can also turn off Night mode completely here.

3. Take the photo normally, but don't move the camera.

Take Apple Proraw Photos

To take pictures in Apple ProRAW, you can use Camera. Apple ProRAW takes the data from a standard RAW format and adds iPhone image processing to give you more creative freedom when you adjust the white balance, exposure, and color.

All of the cameras, even the front camera, can use Apple ProRAW. In Portrait view, Apple ProRAW can't be used.

Setting up Apple proRAW

To use Apple ProRAW or ProRAW & Resolution Control, go to Settings > Camera > Formats and turn them on.

Note: Apple ProRAW photos have bigger file sizes because they keep more details about the images.

Using Apple ProRAW to take a photo

1. Open the Camera and press ⬚ RAW ⬚ or ⬚ RAW MAX ⬚ to turn on ProRAW.
2. Take your shot.

You can switch between ⬚ RAW ⬚ and ⬚ RAW ⬚ or ⬚ RAW MAX ⬚ and ⬚ RAW MAX ⬚ to turn ProRAW on and off while you shoot.

To preserve your ProRAW setting, go to Settings ⬚ > Camera > Preserve Settings, then turn on Apple ProRAW or ProRAW & Resolution Control.

Change apple proRAW resolution

1. Open the camera app 📷.

When your iPhone identifies a person, dog, or cat, ⨍ shows up at the bottom of the viewfinder.

Note: Your iPhone records depth information when⨍ appears while you take a picture in Photo mode. This means that you can add the portrait effect to the photo later in the Photos app 🌸 if you decide not to do it at the time of the shot.

2. If ⨍ doesn't show up, tap a subject in the viewfinder to make it stand out, and it will. Tap a different subject in the viewfinder to change where the portrait's center is.

3. Tap ⨍, then tap the Shutter button to take the photo with the portrait effect.

Note: You can use **photographic styles** on images you take in photo mode.

CHAPTER 5

Video Recording

Record Video

Step 1: To begin, just open the camera program.

Step 2: Swipe up from the bottom of the screen to go to video mode.

Step 3: Press or pick the record button (the big red circle) or one of the volume buttons to start recording. By pressing the white shutter button, you can take a still photo, or you can zoom in and out while the video is being recorded by pinching the screen with two fingers.

Step 4: Press the record button or any of the volume buttons to end the recording.

Action Mode

In this setting, you can record smooth video while moving quickly. Think of it as a very steady movie that you would normally make with just your iPhone and a gimbal.

To turn this mode on, just put your phone in video mode. There will be a new icon at the top. The shape looks like a man running. You can move around while still recording smooth video when it's turned on.

In Action Mode, the movie is cropped a little and has a highest resolution of 2.8K. The crop is needed for your phone to perform post-shoot stabilization.

This mode needs a lot of light, but there is a setting that lets you use it when there isn't much light. The stabilizing impact won't be as strong with this on.

Record a QuickTake video

You can make a special kind of video called QuickTake video while you are in Photo mode. If you swipe the record button left or right while recording the QuickTake video, you can set the lock setting.

These steps will show you how to make a QuickTake video.

Step 1: Open your phone's Camera app.

Step 2: Swipe up from the bottom of the screen to go to Photo mode. Once you're ready to record, press and hold the white camera button.

Step 3: Move the record button to the right to get a lock position or hands-free recording. When you're making a QuickTake movie, click or press the capture button to take still pictures.

Step 4: Click the "Stop" button to end the recording.

Slow motion video

1. Start up the camera app

To open the **Camera** app, tap it.

Tip: If you deleted the Camera app from your phone's Home Screen by accident, swipe left until you get to the App Library and type "Camera" into the search field. You can also scroll up and down to look through the list by letter, then tap Camera to open the app.

2. Swipe to slo-mo mode

The bottom of the screen will show a choice with different ways to record.

Choose **Slo-mo** mode to shoot a clip in slow motion. You can zoom in and out of a slow-motion movie just like any other video.

The front camera can record in Slo-mo mode. For instance, you can record slofies (selfies taken in slow motion) to make movies that will get people's attention on social media and keep them there.

To use the front-facing camera, tap the **Rotate** icon. To take a video, tap the Slo-mo mode icon.

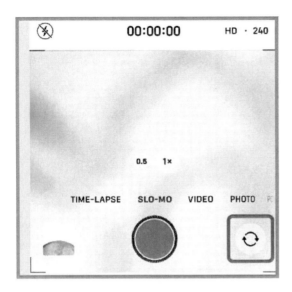

3. Pick the best frame rate

The iPhone camera records videos at 30FPS by default. You can pick from different frame rates and video resolutions, such as 120FPS at 1080p HD or 24, 30, or 60FPS for 4K movies.

4. Plan your shot

Focus on the subject you want to record.

For better slow-motion videos:

- Keep your phone steady while recording; if you can, use a stand. In the end, the recording will show that even small movements can change the focus and make things blurry.

- When shooting small things, stay close, but when shooting big things, move farther away.
- Also, make sure the surface of any glass you're shooting through is clean before you start the video.

5. Hit record

If you want to record your video, press the red Shutter button or any sound button.

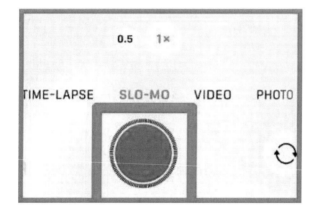

Convert normal video to slo-mo

The Slo-Mo camera effect makes things move more slowly while you record a movie. It moves a lot more slowly than it does in front of you.

Your regular video can be turned into a Slo-Mo movie with the help of a free online app called Clideo. The steps below will show you how to change a regular movie into a Slo-Mo video.

1. Use your iPhone to make a normal video and share it. Open **Video Speed Changer** by Clideo in any browser on your phone.
2. Make the movie move more slowly. Pick any of the speed patterns from 0.25x to 2x. People can also use "Mute video" to turn off the sound of the video.
3. Save a copy of the slow-motion movie. Watch the video to make sure everything is okay. It's up to you if you still want to make changes. If not, click **"Download"** and save.

Record time-lapse video

Take pictures at set times to make a time-lapse video of something happening over time, like the sun going down or traffic moving.

1. Start up the Camera and choose **Time-lapse mode**.
2. Place your iPhone where you want to take a picture of something moving.

3. Press the Record button once to start recording and tap it again to stop.

Record proRes video

You can record and edit movies in ProRes on the iPhone 15's camera. This format has better color accuracy and less compression.

All cameras, even the front camera, can handle ProRes. In panoramic, time-lapse, or slow-motion modes, ProRes can't be used.

ProRes videos have bigger file sizes. Only the 128GB iPhone models can record in 1080p at 30 frames per second. Other than those, ProRes can record in up to 4K at 30 frames per second.

Setup ProRes

- To set up ProRes, go to **Settings > Camera > Formats** and turn on Apple ProRes.

How to record video with ProRes

Follow these steps to record video with ProRes:

- Open the camera, choose video mode, and then press the **ProRes Off button**.

- To start recording, press the Record button or tap one of the sound buttons. When shooting with the back camera, you can pinch or touch to zoom in or out. Press and hold the lens choice and move the dial to get better zoom control.
- If you want to stop recording, press the record button or one of the volume buttons.
- Press the ProRes On button to turn off ProRes.

Record Cinematic video

The depth-of-field effect in cinematic mode keeps the subject of your video clear while blurring the center and background in a beautiful way. The iPhone automatically finds the video's subject and keeps it in focus while the recording is going. If a new subject is found, the iPhone changes the point of focus automatically. You can also change the point of focus by hand while you record or in the Photos app afterward.

1. Startup Camera and choose **Cinematic mode.**

You can tap 3 next to 1x before recording to zoom in.
If you have an iPhone 15, you can pinch the screen to zoom in and out.

Before you record, tap ⓕ and pull the slider left or right to change the depth-of-field effect.

2. To start recording, press either of the volume buttons or tap the Record button.

- If there is a person on the screen, a yellow frame means they are in focus. If there is a gray frame, it means the person was found but is not in focus. If you tap the gray box, you can change the focus. If you tap it again, you can lock the focus on that person.

- If the video doesn't show a person, tap anywhere on the screen to make it the main screen.

- Hold down on the screen to fix the focus on a certain point.

3. To stop recording, press either of the volume buttons or tap the Record button.

How to record the screen

Making a video with the sound of your Apple iPhone 15 screen can be very helpful for making a tutorial or showing an old friend how to do certain things on an

Apple iPhone 15. You can save the video as a file, send it to someone, or post it on a social media site.

If we want to remember or use as proof something, we might want to record an Instagram story, a phone call, or FaceTime video chat with a family member, or a TikTok video.

To make this recording on your Apple iPhone 15, follow these steps:

1. First, we need to make sure that our iPhone 15's screen recording feature is turned on. To check it, press the gear icon on the home screen of your Apple iPhone 15 which is known as Settings.

2. Find the **"Control Center"** section on the left-hand screen and click on **"Customize controls."**

3. If we check the box to record our screen, it will appear in the first list under "INCLUDE" on our iPhone 15. On the right side of the control, there are three horizontal lines that we can click and drag to move it up or down the list. Another way to get rid of the control is to press the red button on the left.

4. If the current control doesn't show, scroll down and it will show up in the **"MORE CONTROLS"** section. Click the **green + button** to add it.

5. If you don't want to use the microphone on your Apple iPhone 15, press the recording button. There will be a 3-second countdown, and then the recording will start. At the top of the screen, a red line and the word "Recording" will show up. This means that everything that happens on the screen is being taped.

6. If you want to record a video with the microphone in addition to the sound from the iPhone 15, you can press and hold the button on the microphone to turn it on or off, then press and hold the button that says **"Start recording."** This could be done to show a friend how to use an app or to record a message while recording the video from the iPhone 15. **Take note: There will be a 3-second timer.**

7. Stop recording by pressing the stop button or clicking on the red line in the top status bar and pressing **"Stop."**

8. The video of you recording the screen has been saved to "Photos," according to a message at the top of your Apple iPhone 15 screen.

Trim video length and adjust slow motion on iPhone

People with iPhones can cut videos down and change the settings for slow motion.

In the Photos app, you can change where a movie on your iPhone starts and ends. You can pick which part of a video to watch slowly when you record in Slo-mo.

How to trim a video

- Open the video in Photos, then pick **Edit** to trim it.
- Move either end of the frame viewer below the video to change the beginning and finish times. Then, press **"Done."**
- In the video player, click **Save Video** to save both versions. You can also click **Save Video as New Clip** to save only the shorter version.

After you save the video, open it and choose **Edit**. Then, choose **Revert** to undo the edit.

There is no way to get a movie back to how it was before if it was saved as a new clip.

Modify the slow-motion portion of a video captured in Slo-mo mode

- Open the video that was recorded in slow-motion mode and tap **Edit.**

- Drag the white bars under the frame viewer to change where the slow-motion movie plays.

CHAPTER 6

Change Camera Settings

Hidden camera settings

Exposure Control: If you put your finger anywhere on the screen, the camera will focus on that spot and the exposure level will be set based on how bright it is there. Just swipe up or down to change the brightness. There is an exposure slider that moves when you move your finger over it.

Focus and Exposure Lock: Hold down the focus point until a yellow box with AE/AF Lock shows up. Now you can move the camera around and the focus and exposure will stay the same. To change the focus and exposure, tap anywhere on the screen.

Camera Settings You Didn't Know About

Take a moment to look at these:

1. Click on Settings.
2. Go to the bottom of the page and tap Photos and Camera.
3. Scroll down until you see "Camera."

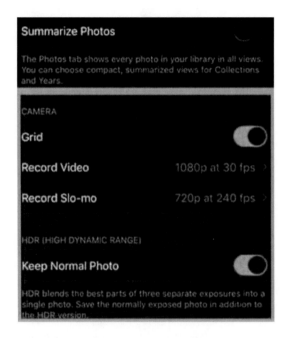

Summarize Photos

The Photos tab shows every photo in your library in all views. You can choose compact, summarized views for Collections and Years.

CAMERA

Grid

Record Video   1080p at 30 fps ›

Record Slo-mo   720p at 240 fps ›

HDR (HIGH DYNAMIC RANGE)

Keep Normal Photo

HDR blends the best parts of three separate exposures into a single photo. Save the normally exposed photo in addition to the HDR version.

Below are your options:

Grid: This puts a grid over the lens. Even though it won't show up in the end image, it's very helpful for lining up shots.

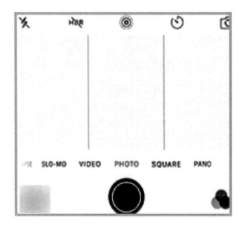

Record Videos: There are 4 ways to record video: 720P at 30fps, 1080P at 30fps, 1080P at 60fps, and 4K at 30fps. It takes up more space on your iPhone as the quality goes up. At 60fps, there should be less blur when moving, but you need more light to get a good picture. Only if you're going to watch it on a computer that can display a 4K image, 4K provides an outstanding image.

Record Slo-Mo: You can choose to record in 1080P at 120 frames per second or 720P at 240 frames per second. You can choose between quality/resolution and speed here. Either one will work well most of the time, but 720P at 240fps makes things move much more slowly. It's important to try new things. There isn't a single setting that is best for everything.

You have one choice in the HDR (High Dynamic Range) section:

Keep Normal Photo: When this is turned on, both the normally exposed photo and the HDR image, which is made up of three different exposures, are saved.

Adjust the Shutter Volume

There will be times when you want to turn off the sound that your iPhone's camera makes. That sound is very annoying when taking pictures at night or in a quiet place, and it doesn't add anything useful to the experience. The sound of the image doesn't do much either.

If you flip the Silent Switch on your iPhone, you can block out the sounds of the camera and screen recording.

To silence the camera on any type of iPhone 15, all you have to do is flick the mute button on the side of the phone. This is the easiest and fastest way to do it. Every iPhone has a switch in the upper left corner that lets you switch between the sound and the quiet mode.

Because it is set to "quiet mode," your iPhone will not make any noise when it gets a call or other message. If you put the shake slider on the Silent position in **Settings > Sounds & Haptics > Vibrate on the Silent slider**, it will still shake even when the volume is lowered. Making sure your iPhone is in quiet mode is very important so that the camera and picture sounds don't play.

When the switch on your phone is closer to the screen, the ring mode is turned on. In other words, your device will play sounds like it normally would. When the switch is in the "quiet" position, the area below it will be orange. If you simply move the switch to the silent position (away from your phone's screen), you can take an endless number of screenshots and images without making a sound.

If you want to silence your iPhone's shutter sound, turn on Live Photos

Any iPhone model that came out after the iPhone 6s can take Live Photos. These so-called **"moving photos"** are made up of a short video clip and sound from before and after the user took the picture. The camera sound will not play on your iPhone if Live Photos is turned on. There would be no point in the Live Photo because you could hear the camera sound in it.

If you want to turn on or off Live Photos in the Camera app, tap the button that looks like a circle with many rings around it. The icon can be found in the top right corner of the screen on most modern devices. If the icon does not have a slash through it, Live Photos is turned on. When you take a picture, you will not hear a shutter sound.

Because of this feature, you can turn off the camera sound on your iPhone without having to stop it. Using this method to take photos will not, however, turn off the sound effects.

It is important to remember that Live Photos take up more space on your phone and could include sounds that you don't want other people to hear.

HDR Camera Settings

You can take beautiful shots in places with a lot of contrast if you have an HDR camera. The iPhone takes several pictures quickly, each with a different exposure. These pictures are then put together to make the highlights and shadows clearer in your photos.

If HDR is turned on, the iPhone will take pictures with both its front-facing and back-facing cameras.

Disable automatic HDR

HDR is used by default on the iPhone when it's most useful. Some iPhone models let you change the HDR settings by hand.

To turn off Smart HDR,

- Go to Settings > Camera.
- On the camera's display, tap **HDR** to turn it on or off.
- Press **HDR** and then "On" to turn HDR back on for the camera's screen.

Keep a photo's non-HDR version

Photos automatically save the HDR version of a photo. The version that doesn't have HDR can also be saved on iPhones older than the X.

- Go to **Settings > Camera** and choose **"Keep Normal Photo"** from the drop-down box.

Activate and deactivate HDR video

You can get true colors and contrast when you record video on an iPhone in Dolby Vision HDR. To stop taking HDR videos, go to **Settings > Camera > Record Video** and turn off HDR Video.

Change Video Recording Settings

It captures video at 30 frames per second (fps) by default. You can pick a different movie resolution and frame rate. Video files get bigger when the frame rate and quality go up.

You can also quickly switch between video resolutions and frame rates right on the camera screen.

Use quick toggles to change video resolution and frame rate

Switch between the different video resolutions and frame rates on your iPhone quickly at the top of the screen when you're in Video mode.

You can choose between HD or 4K video and 24, 25, 30, or 60 frames per second in Video mode by tapping the quick toggles in the upper right corner.

Adjourn the Auto FPS settings

When there isn't much light, the iPhone can instantly lower the frame rate to 24 fps to improve the quality of the video.

Click on **Camera** > **Record Video** in the settings menu 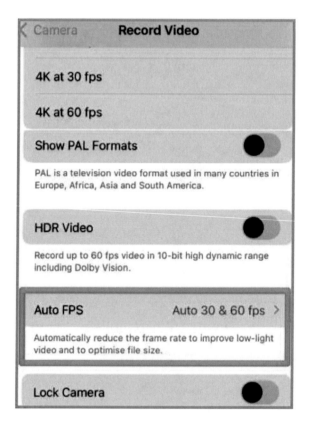.

Press "Auto FPS" and pick the choice you want.

Turn stereo recording on or off

1. Go to **Settings** on your iPhone.

2. Go to the **Camera**.

3. Turn on the choice for **stereo sound**.

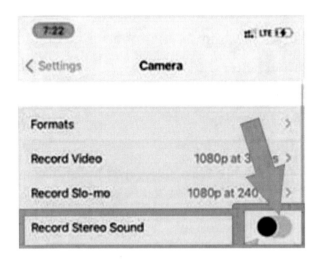

When you turn on stereo sound for videos on your iPhone, both microphones will pick up music. For stereo sound, the microphone at the bottom will pick up the right channel, and the microphone on the camera will pick up the left channel.

Activate Lock Camera

With the Lock Camera setting, the camera won't switch between itself automatically while you're taking video. At first, the Lock Camera is turned off.

Go to Settings > Camera > Record Video and then turn on Lock Camera.

Enhances stabilization

The Enhanced Stabilization setting zooms in a little to make stabilization better when shooting in Video mode and Cinematic mode. By default, Enhanced Stabilization is turned on.

Go to Settings > Camera > Record Video and then turn off Enhanced Stabilization.

Save camera settings on iPhone

Here's what you can do to save your iPhone 15's camera settings:

1. On your iPhone, open the Settings app.
2. Find **Camera** and tap it.
3. Click on **Preserve Settings**.
4. You will see a list of choices that you can select to save the changes. Some of these are:
   - **Camera Mode**: Save the last camera mode you used, like Video or Pano.

- **Creative Controls:** When you use the filter, lighting option, or depth control, save the last changes you made.
- **Macro Control:** Leave the Auto Macro setting alone so that the Ultra Wide camera doesn't take photos and videos of macro subjects by itself.
- **Exposure Adjustment:** Save the value for the exposure control.
- **Night Mode:** Save the setting for Night Mode instead of going back to Auto.
- **Portrait Zoom:** Save the zoom in Portrait mode instead of going back to the original lens.
- **Action Mode:** Don't turn off the Action Mode setting. Instead, leave it on.
- **Apple ProRAW:** Save the setting for Apple ProRAW.
- **Apple ProRes:** Keep the setting for Apple ProRes.
- **Live Photo:** Save the setting for Live Photo.

Now, when you open your iPhone camera again, your choices will still be there. Enjoy taking pictures with the settings you like! 📷

Advanced Camera Settings

View Outside the Frame

1. On your iPhone, open the Settings app.

2. Find Camera and tap it.

3. Go to the settings menu and scroll down until you find the Composition area.

4. Use the toggle to enable **View Outside the Frame**.

Prioritize Faster Shooting

When you quickly press the Shutter button, the Prioritize Faster Shooting setting changes the way pictures are processed to allow you to take more photos. Prioritize Faster Shooting is already turned on by default.

Go to Settings > Camera and turn off Prioritize Faster Shooting.

Lens Correction

The Lens Correction setting makes photos taken with the front camera or Ultra Wide camera look more like they were taken in real life. Lens Correction is always on.

Go to Settings > Camera and turn off Lens Correction.

Scene Detention

With the Scene Detection setting, your camera can figure out what you're photographing and give it a specific look that brings out the best in it. Scene Detection is always on.

Go to Settings > Camera and turn off Scene Detection.

CHAPTER 7

Use Live Text

Utilize Live Text with the camera

With the Camera app, you can copy and share text that shows up on the camera screen, as well as browse websites, write emails, and make calls.

1. The first step is to launch the Camera app on your iPhone and then position it so that the text is visible in the photo.

2. When the text you want to use has a yellow border around it, click the Live Text choice.

3. Move the text around or use grab points to pick it, and then do one of the following:

- **Copy Text:** If you want to put text into another app, like Notes or Messages, you can copy it and paste it there.

- **Choose All:** Pick out all of the words in the frame.

- **Look Up:** Google words to find it.

- **Translate:** The text needs to be translated.

- **Share:** You can share text through Mail, AirDrop, or Messages, among other ways.

4. To call, visit a website, or send an email, tap the phone number, email address, or website on the screen.

5. To turn on the camera, press the **Live Text On button.**

Scaning QR codes

You can scan Quick Response (QR) codes with your camera or a code reader to get to deals, websites, apps, tickets, and more. The camera sees a QR code right away and marks it.

Use the camera to scan QR codes

- Open the camera on your iPhone, then put it where the barcode will show up on the screen.
- Tap the displayed message to go to the website or app you want to use.

Launch Code Scanner via the Control Center

- Go to Settings > Control Center menu and click the **Insert button** next to Code Scanner.
- Go to **Control Center**, tap **Code Scanner**, and move the iPhone so the barcode shows up on the screen.
- Press the flashlight button to make it brighter.

CHAPTER 8

View And Share Photos

View your Photos

You can sort the movies and photos on your device by Years, Months, Days, and All Photos in the Library. You can relive past events by looking at some of your best photos in Years, remembering important events in Months, focusing on unique photos in Days, and seeing all of your images in All Photos.

Click on the Library tab and choose one of the following groups to look through your photos:

All Photos: You can view every movie or image on your device, and you can also zoom in or out by pinching the screen with two fingers.

Years: For each year, choose it from your library and then watch the movie that shows important events that happened that year.

Days: You can look at your pictures grouped by time or place.

Months: Look through a collection of pictures taken during the month, organized by events like a family trip, wedding, graduation, or trip.

1. While Viewing a photo tap 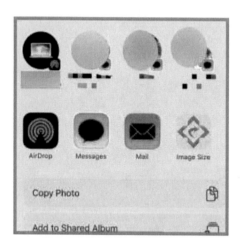.

2. Pick a way to share your photos, like AirDrop, Mail, or Messages.

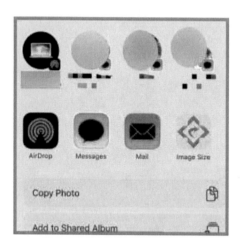

3. Select Print from the list of actions to print your photo by swiping it up.

Upload your photos and keep them up to date across all your device

You can upload photos and videos from your iPhone to iCloud with iCloud Photos and then view them on other devices that are signed in with the same Apple ID. This is helpful if you want to save space on your iPhone or make sure that all of your devices have the most up-to-date photos. To make iCloud Photos work, go to Settings and then Photos.

CHAPTER 9

Print Out Form From Iphone 15
Before you begin

- Make sure that AirPrint works with your printer. Get more information from the company that made your printer.
- Make sure that both your printer and your iPhone or iPad are on the same Wi-Fi network and that you can reach each other.

Print with AirPrint

1. Start up the app you want to print from.

2. Tap the Share button 🔙 **or** ⬆️ or the Actions button in the app to find the print button.

3. Find the Print button 🖨️ or Print and press it. Check the app's User Guide or Help area if you can't find the print button. Not every app works with AirPrint.

4. Tap "No Printer Selected" and pick a printer that works with AirPrint.

5. You can pick the pages you want to print or the number of copies you want.

6. In the top right corner, click Print.

How to print via email

You can print emails from your iPhone in two main ways: first, you can use AirPrint to print the email directly from your iPhone; second, you can use a computer to do it. Pick one of these ways based on what you need to do.

Method 1 - Print an Email from iPhone with AirPrint

As you may know, the iPhone, iPad, iPod Touch, and Mac all come with AirPrint, which lets you print pictures and documents right from your device. If you want to print an email from your iPhone, you might want to use AirPrint.

What you need to do to use AirPrint to print an email from your iPhone:

- You can connect both your iPhone and the printer to the same Wi-Fi network.
- The printer is AirPrint-supported. (Make sure it does.)
- You can use AirPrint with the app you want to print emails from.

Read these steps to learn how to use AirPrint to print an email from your iPhone.

Step 1: Open Mail on your iPhone and tap "Inbox."

Step 2: Click on the email you want to print. Tap the **Forward icon** at the bottom of your iPhone screen and select **Print**.

Step 3: Go to the **Printer Options** page and pick the printer you want to print the email to. You can choose a Canon, Brother, KODAK, or other printer. You can also choose how many copies you want to make and the page range.

Step 4: To print an iPhone email, tap **Print** in the upper right corner of the screen.

There are two ways to print emails from your iPhone: Method 2 or Method 1. If AirPrint isn't working, you can fix the problem first and then use Method 1.

Method 2: Print Emails from your iPhone without AirPrint

AirPrint is one way to print emails from an iPhone, but it's not the only way. If you have iCloud and a computer, you can print your emails. These are the easy steps you need to take.

Step 1: Go to **Settings > [your name] > iCloud** on your iPhone and turn on Mail.

Step 2: Open a browser on your computer and go to **iCloud.com**. Then, use your Apple ID and password to sign in.

Step 3: Click on **Mail** and then on the email you want to print.

Step 4: In the bottom left corner of the screen, tap the gear button. Then, choose **Print.**

Step 5: Choose how you want to print, then click **"Print"** to print Emails from your iPhone without AirPrint.

Take note:

If you want to print the photos or other things that can be found in your email. You can either download photos to your iPhone and print them, or you can move photos from your iPhone to your computer and print them from there.

How to print with Goggle Cloud Print
Step 1: Download the app you want to use

- Google Docs
- Google Sheets
- Google Slides

Step 2: Set up printing on your computer

Step 3: Use your phone to print.

1. Open the Google Docs, Sheets, or Slides app on your iPhone or iPad.
2. Press "More" ⋯ on the file you want to print.
3. Click **Share & export** ⟩ Print 🖶.
4. Tap **Google Cloud Print** next to "Print."
5. To choose the printer, follow the instructions given.
6. Press the Print button 🖶.

CHAPTER 10

Set Up Facetime on Iphone
How to use FaceTime

You can make both voice and video calls with FaceTime. To do this, you use Wi-Fi or a cell phone network. You can also FaceTime with a group. You have to turn on FaceTime before you can use it. So, either open the **FaceTime** app or go to **Settings** and choose **FaceTime.** Then use your Apple ID to sign in. However, FaceTime will already have your phone number saved.

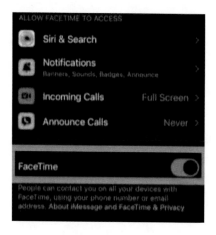

Make a FaceTime call

Before you can make a FaceTime call, you need to have the other person's phone number or registered email address. Choose **"New FaceTime"** when you open the app. Type the person's phone number or email address in the box that says **"To: "**

Type in the address or number. Click on the audio button to make a call. Click on the video button (FaceTime) to make a video call.

During a call, you can choose to start FaceTime with the other person right away. Just press the FaceTime link in the Phone app.

How to Answer a FaceTime audio call with call waiting

When you are on a call, and another person calls you maybe a FaceTime or Phone call. What you can do is one of three things.

1. If you want to answer the new call, you can end the call you are on now.
2. The caller can choose to be put on hold while you answer the new call.
3. You can decide not to answer the phone when it rings.

How to use Memoji on FaceTime

Tap on the screen and choose the **star icon** below the screen while you're on a FaceTime call. That's the icon for **Effects**. It's that easy. Just click the Memoji button and pick out the one you want to use. You can pick out a Memoji by scrolling to the right.

It will show up on your face during FaceTime after you choose one. Click the "None" **(X)** button to close or delete the Memoji.

Begin a FaceTime Audio/Video call from messages

You can begin a FaceTime call with the person you're talking with in an iMessage.

1. Press ▇◀ in the upper right corner of the iMessage chat.
2. Do any of these things:

- Click on FaceTime Audio.
- Click on FaceTime Video.

Leave a message

People you know will be asked to leave a voicemail if they don't answer your FaceTime call if you're a known friend of that person (either you're in their Contacts or you've recently messaged or called them).

If the person you're calling has Live Voicemail turned on in Settings > Phone, your message will be typed out on their screen as you talk. This lets them know why you're calling and gives them a chance to pick up.

Call back

Do any of these things to call someone back on FaceTime:

- On the Record Video screen, tap Call Again.
- Go to your call records and tap on the name or number of the person or group you want to call again.

Get a link to a FaceTime call

You can make a link to a FaceTime call in FaceTime and send it to a friend or a group of friends through Mail or Messages. They can join or start a call with the link.

1. To make a link, open the FaceTime app and tap Create Link near the top of the screen.
2. Pick a way to send the link, like email, text message, etc.

Take a live photos with FaceTime

You can take a FaceTime Live Photo during a video call in the FaceTime app to remember a part of the chat (not available everywhere). What happens before and after you take the photo is recorded by the camera, along with the sound, so you can see and hear it later exactly as it happened.

First, go to Settings > FaceTime and make sure that FaceTime Live Photos is turned on. Then, do one of the following:

*   *On a call with one other person*: Tap.

- *On a Group FaceTime call:* Tap the tile of the person you want to snap, tap , then tap .

You both receive a notification that the photo was taken. The Live Photo is saved in your Photos app.

Turn on live captions for FaceTime calls on iPhone

You can turn on Live Captions during a FaceTime video call to see the spoken chat as text on your iPhone in real-time. Live Captions can help you follow along if you're having trouble hearing what's being said.

It is important to remember that Live Captions aren't always accurate, so you shouldn't depend on them in dangerous or emergency circumstances. Live Captions needs more battery power.

1. Tap the screen during a FaceTime video call to see the settings if you can't see them.

2. At the top of the screen, tap to turn on Live Captions. Then, tap "Done" to finish.

A "Live Captions" window pops up near the top of the screen. It shows the automatically transcribed call conversation and who is talking.

To turn off Live Captions, tap the screen, then tap  at the top of the FaceTime controls. This will hide the transcript of the chat.

Using other apps during FaceTime calls

The FaceTime app  lets you use other apps at the same time. For example, you can use one to look something up, write a note, or do math.

To open an app, go to the Home Screen and tap on an icon.

Tap the green bar (or the FaceTime icon) at the top of the screen to go back to the FaceTime screen.

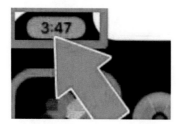

You can also use another app and share your screen with the other people on your FaceTime call.

Start a Group FaceTime call from the FaceTime app

1. Get on Messages and start a chat with a group. Or join a group chat that's already going on.
2. In the top right corner, tap the FaceTime button .
3. Press on either FaceTime Audio or FaceTime Video .

A Group FaceTime call can have up to 32 people.

Start a Group FaceTime call from the Messages app

1. Make sure FaceTime is on by going to Settings > FaceTime.
2. Tap New FaceTime when you open FaceTime.
3. Put in the names of the people you want to call.
4. You can also press the FaceTime or Audio button .

A Group FaceTime call can have up to 32 people.

Let's Join a Group FaceTime call
After someone starts a Group FaceTime call, you can join in a few different ways:

- Open the Notification Center or the Lock screen and tap the message. Then, tap the FaceTime button ▣.

- It's easy to join a Group FaceTime call from Messages. Just tap the notification at the top of the screen or tap Join in the group chat. As soon as you press **"Join,"** you're linked.

- To join a call from the FaceTime app, just tap the FaceTime button ▣ next to the call that's already going on.

Adding someone to a FaceTime group call
- In the call, tap the people who are already there, then tap "Add People ⊕."
- Type in their name, phone number, or email address.
- Press "Add People."

To make sure the person you're calling knows about the call, you can tap the "Ring" button next to their name. This will make their device ring again.

When someone joins a Group FaceTime call, they can't be taken off of it. That person needs to end the Group FaceTime call on their device to leave the call.

View participants in a grid in FaceTime on an iPhone

When you're on a FaceTime call with four or more people, you can see everyone in a grid of tiles of the same size. The speaker's tile stands out on its own, making it easy to see who is speaking.

Tap the Grid button in the bottom left corner of the screen during a FaceTime call. If you can't see the button, tap the screen.

Tap the button again to turn off the grid.

Watch and listen together in FaceTime on iPhone with Shareplay

You can stream TV shows, movies, and songs with friends and family while on a FaceTime call with SharePlay in the FaceTime app. With shared controls and synced audio, you can connect with other people on the call in real-time. You can see and hear the same things at the same time. With smart volume, the sound in your media is changed on the fly, so you can still talk while you watch or listen. You can also play online games that work with Game Center with friends while they are on FaceTime.

During a FaceTime call, you can also use SharePlay in other apps. Tap and then read through the apps below **Apps for SharePlay** to see which ones can be used for SharePlay during a call.

Note: You may need to pay for some apps that work with SharePlay. All people who want to watch a movie or TV show together must have access to it on their device, either through a subscription or a buy, and that device must meet certain system requirements.

Some movies and TV shows might not be able to be shared between countries or regions on SharePlay. Some countries or areas may not be able to use FaceTime or some of its features. Other Apple services may also not be available.

During a FaceTime call, you and your family and friends can watch movies and TV shows at the same time.

1. Use the FaceTime app on your iPhone to start a call.

2. Tap , then tap an app (like the Apple TV app) below Listen and Play Together.

You can also open a video streaming app that works with SharePlay from the Home Screen.

3. To watch a show or movie with everyone on the call, choose one, press the **"Play"** button, and then "Play for Everyone" if it shows up. (Some people on the call might need to tap **Join SharePlay** to watch the video.)

The movie starts playing at the same time for everyone on the call who can see it. As a way to get access, people who don't have it are asked to subscribe, buy something, or try it out for free, if possible.

Each person watching can use the controls to play, stop, rewind, or fast-forward the video. (Each person has their power over things like closed captioning and volume.)

Inviting friends to watch videos together with supported apps during a FaceTime call

1. Find a movie or show you want to share in the Apple TV app or another video app that works with it. Then, tap on it to see more information about it.

2. Press and then press SharePlay.

3. Type the names of the people you want to share with in the "To" field, then press "FaceTime."

4. Tap Start or Play to start using SharePlay when the FaceTime call comes in.

People who receive it tap "Open" to start watching.

Note: If the video needs a subscription, people who don't have one can sign up before watching.

Cast what you're watching on Share play to your Apple TV

Once you're both into a movie on your iPhone, you can send it to your Apple TV to watch on a bigger screen.

One of these things should be done on your iPhone:

- Press ▣ in the streaming app, then pick Apple TV as the place to play.

- Open Control Center, tap ▣, and then pick Apple TV as the place to play.

The Apple TV plays the video at the same time, and you can talk on your iPhone.

Listen to music together during a FaceTime call

1. Start a FaceTime call with a group.

2. Press ▣, then tap one of the music apps below Listen and Play Together, like with the Apple TV app ▣. You can also open a music streaming app that supports SharePlay from the Home Screen. The Music app is one option ▣.

3. You can then choose the music you want to listen to and press the "Play" button to start. (Some people on the call might need to tap Join SharePlay to hear the music.)

The music starts playing at the same time for everyone on the call who can hear it. As a way to get access, people who don't have it are asked to subscribe, buy something, or try it out for free, if possible.

You can stop, rewind, fast-forward, scrub to a different part of the song, or go to the next track with the music controls. The shared queue can have songs added by anyone on the call.

Invite friends to listen to music together from supported apps during a FaceTime call

1. Start the Apple Music app or any other music app that works with this one. 2. Tap the song you want to share.

2. Pick one of these things:

    • Press next to the song, then tap **SharePlay**.

    • Press in the upper right corner, tap , and then press **SharePlay.**

3. Next, type the names of the people you want to share with in the "To" field. Finally, tap "FaceTime."

4. Press **Start** when the FaceTime call starts.

People who receive the music must first tap the song title at the top of the FaceTime settings and then tap

"Open" to start listening. The music starts playing at the same time for everyone on the call who can hear it.

Please note that people who can't see the information you share are asked to do so.

Start sharing your screen

1. If you can't see the FaceTime settings during a call in the FaceTime app ▇ on your iPhone, tap the screen and then tap ▇.

2. Tap Share My Screen to show your whole screen to other people.

There is a countdown from three to one on ▇, and then a small image of your screen shows up in the FaceTime call. The people on the call can tap it to make it bigger and see what you're saying.

Tap ▇ to stop sharing your screen.

1. While the iPhone is on a FaceTime call, do one of the things below on the other iPad:

   - Tap the message that says "Move call to this [device]."

   - Press the screen's top button.

You can see your camera, microphone, and audio options in a preview of the call.

2. Make sure the settings are right, then press Join or Switch.

The call is sent to the new phone. A logo and a Switch button show up on the original device to let you know that the call continued somewhere else. You can tap the button to bring the callback.

Blurring the background using portrait mode

1. On your iPhone, open the Photos app .

2. Tap any Photo mode photo to see it in full screen, then tap Edit.

3. If there are portrait effects, tap and then tap Portrait at the top of the screen.

4. Turn up or down the Depth Control slider to change how blurry the background is in the picture.

5. Press "Done."

Click on the photo, then on Edit, and then on Revert to undo the portrait effects.

Note: You can't use the Live Photo effects on a Live Photo that was taken in Photo mode with the portrait effect. If you tap Live, you can see the Live Photo or add a Live Photo effect that doesn't have the picture effect.

Change FaceTime audio settings
Isolate Background Sounds on a FaceTime Call

That spatial sound effect might not sound good on your FaceTime call if there is noise in the background. Voice isolation on your iPhone can be used to change this and make the FaceTime call quieter. This is how you do it:

Step 1: Open the FaceTime app and join your FaceTime call.

Step 2: Open Control Center while on the FaceTime call.

Step 3: In the Control Center, tap Mic Mode.

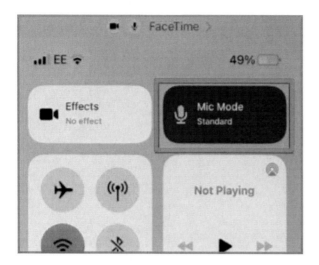

Step 4: Choose Voice Isolation from the list of tabs.

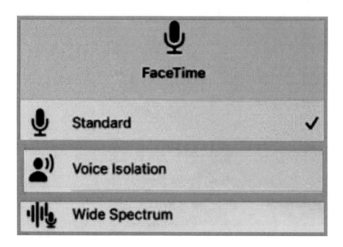

Include Background Sounds on a FaceTime Call

You can turn on Wide Spectrum mode in FaceTime if you want the sounds around you and your words to be sent over. This is how you do it:

Step 1: Open the FaceTime app and join your FaceTime call.

Step 2: Open Control Center while on the FaceTime call.

Step 3: In the Control Center, tap Mic Mode.

Step 4: From the menu, select Wide Spectrum.

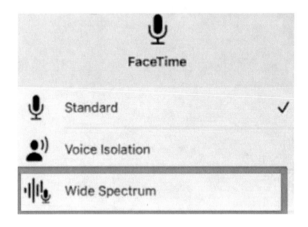

Adding filter effects on FaceTime calls

Step 1: Open the FaceTime app and join the call.

Step 2: During the FaceTime call, find the tile with your image on it and tap it.

Step 3: On the screen, tap the star sign .

Step 4: Click on the icon to see the options.

Step 5: Swipe left or right on the filter choices to select the one you want.

End the FaceTime call

During a FaceTime call, you can get to the menu by tapping anywhere on the screen.

In the upper right spot, press **Leave** or **End.**

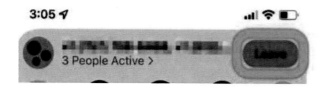

When you are on a FaceTime group call, the button will say **Leave**. When you are on a FaceTime one-on-one call, it will say **End**. That's all there is to it! It's very simple to make sure you hang up the phone when you meant to. This will get you out of any FaceTime call, whether it's with just one person or with a bunch of people.

Join a FaceTime call from your Android or Windows device

Whether you have an Android or Windows phone, you can use your computer to join a FaceTime call. Links are used to do this. With this link, they can use their phone to join the call. They need to use a computer that works with the site to join. Apple says that those browsers are the most recent versions of **Google Chrome, Microsoft Edge,** and other browsers that support **H.264 encoding**.

- To do this, open the FaceTime app first. Select the **"Create Link"** button at the top of the screen.
- There will be a shared page. Pick out a place to send the link. The link can also be copied.

- Now, on your Android phone, click on the link you were sent. A computer browser should be able to open it.
- After that, the page will ask you to add your name to the chat. After typing the name, click **Continue.**
- Then click **Join** in the FaceTime box. After that, wait for the Host to accept you.
- Allow the Android user to join the call on your iPhone by tapping the **Check** button at the top of the FaceTime screen. Press the **"Leave"** button to end the chat.

How to Share Your Screen on a FaceTime Call

When you start a FaceTime call. Pick out the **Share Content button** from the page. After that, choose **Share My Screen**. If you join this way, the people you connect with can see what's on your screen but can't change anything on your iPhone. They can't see the notice when you get it.

Someone else's screen can be shared with you. In a call, all you have to do is press the "Open" button, which is to the left of the "Join Screen Sharing" button.

After someone else shares their screen, click the Share Content button to take over. Just click on Share My Screen and then click on **Replace Existing**. Press the **Share Content button** again to end the screen share.

CHAPTER 11

Apple Photos App

Navigate through the Photo app

1. Open **Photos** on your iPad or iPhone.

2. If you're not already there, tap the **Library** tab in the bottom left area.

3. Choose the **timeline view** you want to see: **Years, Months, Days, or All Photos.**

   - It will go down to **Months** if you start at **Years** and then tap on a year.

   - If you tap on a month in the **Months** view, it changes to the **Days** view.

   - Tapping on an image will display all of the photos from that day.

4. In the menu bar above the Photo tabs, you can exit your current view by tapping on **Years, Months, or Days.**

If you want to go back to the last level, you can swipe from the left edge of your screen. It won't work, though, if you are looking at individual pictures. To go back, you'll need to tap the **back button** in the upper left corner. Swiping will only take you to the previous or next photo.

Tips and tricks for apple photos

How to add text to your pictures on app photos

1. Open the Photos app

To open the Photos app, tap on its icon. The pictures tab is in the bottom left corner of your screen. Tap it to see all of your pictures. On the other hand, you can browse by Albums.

2. Pick out the desired photo

Have you found the desired image? To open it, just tap it.

3. Press the "Edit" button

Find the Edit button in the upper right area of the screen. Next, click the More button, which looks like three dots. You can choose Markup from this point on.

4. Press the plus sign and choose Text.

Press and hold the plus sign (+) in the bottom right corner of the screen. This will show you a list of things to do. Choose Text.

5. Type your message

Just type what you want to add.

6. Make changes

Use the Color button to change the color of your text. Press the aA button (next to the Plus button) to change the font style, size, and/or alignment of the text.

7. Press "Done" twice

Tap **"Done"** in the upper right corner when you're done. In your Photos app, you can now find the text you added to your image.

How to make a picture on one of your favorites in apple photos

1. On your phone, open the **Photos** app.
2. Touch and hold the picture you want to mark as a favorite.
3. Touch the **heart** at the bottom of the screen. Once your picture has been added to Favorites, the heart icon will turn blue.

How to share one or more photos in apple photos

- *Share a single photo or video:* Go to the photo or video, tap , and then pick a way to share it, like Mail, Messages, or AirDrop.
- *Share multiple photos or videos:* If you see a screen with many thumbnails, press Select and

then tap the photos and movies you want to share. Press and pick a way to share, like Mail, Messages, or AirDrop.

- *Share photos or videos from a day or month:* Click on Library, then click on Days or Months. Next, click on and then on Share Photos. Pick a way to share, like Mail, Messages, or AirDrop.

If you have iCloud pictures turned on, you can use an iCloud link to share several high-quality pictures. iCloud links are safe for 30 days, anyone can see them, and any app, like Messages or Mail, can be used to share them.

You can also share pictures and videos with only certain people through Shared Albums.

Note: Your service provider decides how big a file can be. If a service or device doesn't allow Live Photos, they are shared as still photos.

How to delete photos in apple photos

1. Click on Photos.
2. Select the photo or video you want to get rid of by tapping All Photos on the Library tab.

3. Press the "Trash" button 🗑 and then "Delete Photo."

Delete duplicate photos and videos

1. Open the Photos app and tap Albums.
2. Go to Utilities and tap the Duplicates album.
3. Press "Merge" to merge the copies.
4. To make sure, tap Merge [Number] Items.

When you merge duplicate photos, your phone keeps the best image quality and important data from both to make a single photo in your library. The other duplicate pictures will now be in the album called "Recently Deleted."

Recover deleted photos or videos

1. Click on Photos and then on the Albums tab.
2. Go to Utilities and tap the Recently Deleted album.
3. To get into your Recently Deleted album, use Face ID.
4. Press the Select button.

5. Tap Recover after choosing the photo or movie you want to keep. Tap Recover All if you want to get back every photo and video in the album.

6. To be sure, tap **"Recover Photo."**

You can get back a photo or video that you deleted by accident for 30 days from the album called "Recently Deleted." Photos and movies are returned to your Library when you recover them.

Make the Recently Deleted album unlocked by default

1. Open the app called Settings.

2. Click on Photos.

3. Stop using Face ID.

By default, you need Face ID to see the Hidden and Recently Deleted files. If you turn off "Use Face ID," the Hidden file will no longer be locked.

Delete photos permanently

1. Click on Photos and then on the Albums tab.

2. Touch the Recently Deleted album.

3. To get into your Recently Deleted file, use Face ID or Touch ID.

4. Press the Select button.

5. Click the Delete button next to the photo or movie you want to delete. Tap Delete All to clear the album of every photo and video.

6. To be sure, tap Delete Photo.

Image editing

How to crop, flip, and rotate pictures and videos

Let's go over the basics of cropping a picture in case you don't know what it means. A picture is cropped when a piece is cut off of one side or edge. Most of the time, this means trying to keep a certain aspect ratio, like 4:3 or 1:1. There are times, though, when you just want to get rid of something or someone in your picture. You might want a specific shape for your image.

You'll learn how to do most of these things in the Photos app that comes with your iPhone. For some of the more unusual techniques in this piece, you'll need software from a third party. These will be talked about in more depth in the parts that belong to them.

What is the best way to crop a picture to a certain aspect ratio?

Crop your photo in Photos as follows if you want your photo to retain its shape:

1. In the Photos app, find the picture you want to crop.

2. Click on Edit.

3. At the bottom, tap the Crop button.

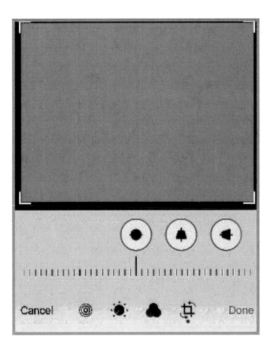

4. Press the Aspect Ratio button just below the three dots in the upper right spot.

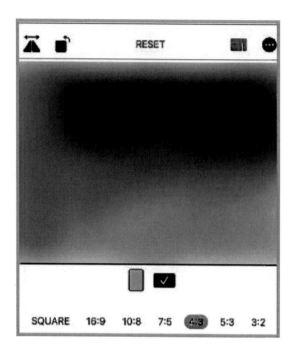

5. Choose the ratio of the image's sides, and then put it inside the box.

6. Click the **"Done"** button.

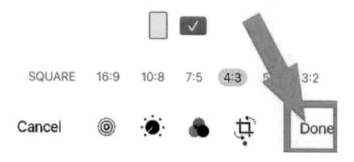

Crop a picture by hand

Maybe you only want to cut something off the side of one of your pictures and don't care about the form factor. What you need to do is this:

1. Locate the photo you want to change in the Photos app.
2. Tap the Crop button at the bottom of the screen.
3. To change the aspect ratio, press the **Aspect Ratio button** in the upper right corner.
4. Start framing your image by selecting Freehand.
5. Click the "Done" button.

On my iPhone, how can I crop a photo into a circle?

To turn pictures into circles, you will need to use software from a different source. Adobe Photoshop Mix, which you can get from the App Store, will be used for this part.

Now that you have the app on your phone, do these things:

1. Get on your computer and open Photoshop Mix.
2. Select the photo you want to crop by choosing Image from the Plus menu.

3. From **Cut Out > Shape**, choose the circle.

4. Move your finger around the picture to make a circle. You could also squeeze it to make it the right size.

5. Tap the checkmark in the bottom right spot.

Change the lighting and color scheme

- To watch a photo or video in full screen, click its thumbnail in Photos.

- Click "Edit," then swipe left on the picture to see the effects you can change. These include "Shadows," "Exposure," "Highlights," and "Brightness."

- Tap the impact you want, and then move the slider to make small changes.

Based on the shape of the button, which shows how much each effect was changed, you can quickly see which effects have been boosted or dropped. Tap the effect button to switch between the changed effect and the original one.

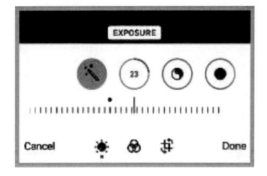

- To save your changes, click **"Done."** If you don't like them, click **"Cancel"** and then **"Discard Changes."**

Note: If you click the Enhance button, effects will be added instantly to your photos or videos.

Crop, rotate, or mirror an image or video

1. In Photos, tap on a thumbnail to see the full picture or video.
2. Click **Edit**
3. When you click ![icon], one of these things should happen:

- **Crop manually**: To crop an image by hand, drag the rectangle's sides to include the part of the picture you want to keep. You can also pinch the picture to open or close it.

- **Crop to a predefined ratio standard:** press the "**Aspect Ratio Freeform**" button and pick a choice like "square," "16:9," or "5:4"
- **Rotate:** To rotate the image by 90 degrees, click the **Rotate** button.
- **Flip**: You can flip an image horizontally by clicking the **Flip** button.

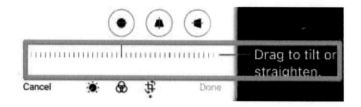

4. Hit **"Done"** to save your changes, or hit "Cancel" and then **"Discard Changes"** if you don't like them.

Adjust and correct your perspective

- To watch a photo or video in full screen, click its thumbnail in Photos.
- Click Edit and then tap ⌗.
- When you swipe left on the image, straighten, vertical, and horizontal effects will appear.
- Tap the effect you want, and then move the slider to make small changes.

If you look at the outline of the button, you can quickly see which effects have been boosted or lowered based on how much change was made. Tap the button to switch between the changed effect and the original one.

- To save your changes, press **"Done."** If you don't like them, press **Cancel** and after that press **"Discard Changes."**

Utilize filtering effects

- To watch a photo or video in full screen, click its thumbnail in Photos.

- Press Edit and then Filters ⊛ to use filter effects like Vivid, Dramatic, or Silvertone.

- Pick a filter and move the impact slider to change it.

To see how the changed photo compares to the original, tap it.

- To save your changes, press **"Done."** If you don't like them, tap **"Cancel"** and then **"Discard Changes."**

How to Revert an altered image

You can go back to the original form of a photo after editing it and saving it.

- Open the image that you changed, then choose Edit, and then Revert.
- Press **"Revert to Default."**

Write or draw on a photograph

- To view a photo in full-screen mode, tap it in Photos.
- Press Edit and then the Mark Up button Ⓐ.
- To annotate the image, use a variety of drawing tools and colors. Use the "Add Annotations" button to make an image bigger or to add a caption, shape, text, or even your signature.
- If you don't like the changes you made, click Cancel instead of Done.

How to Get Rid of Objects in Photos

Step 1: Open the app and pick out a picture from the Albums section.

Step 2: Make the part of the picture you want to get rid of bigger.

Step 3: From the drop-down box, choose **Object Removal**. The brush will be picked out for you. Now, use single, broad strokes to "paint" over the thing. Hit the "Go" button.

Step 4: Get rid of the thing. If there are any strange lines on it, swipe over it again. If you want to undo it, you can tap the Undo button in the top bar.

Step 5: When you're done with the picture, press the Share button and pick Gallery from the choice that comes up. This will save the picture to your Camera Roll.

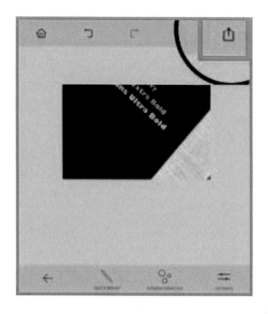

You can pick exact areas with the Lasso tool as well. In the same way, the other Quick Repair and Line Removal options work.

Apple Photo Memory Tips and Ticks

Creating a Memory Movie

1. Tap the **"For You"** tab in Photos.

2. You can scroll through your memories by tapping "See All." To play a memory, tap it once. To see choices, like Memory mixes 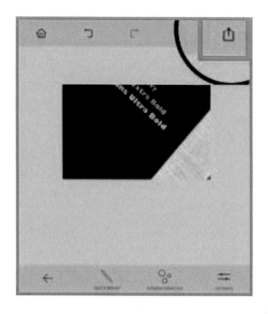 or Browse , tap the memory again. When you press the Browse button , the music will keep

playing while the photos in the memory are shown to you.

Change the Memory mix

Memory mixes are carefully put together groups of photo looks and songs that go with them that you can use for memory. You can pick from different Memory mixes for each memory, or you can use Apple Music to choose your look and song. How to do it:

1. Tap the "For You" tab in Photos.
2. Just tap on a memory to play it.
3. Press the screen, then press the Memory mixes button . To switch between mixes, swipe left on the screen.
4. To use the Memory mix, tap the screen again.

Create your memories

To make your Memories from a certain record, month, or day:

1. Click on the Albums tab and pick out the package. You can also tap Months or Days in the Library tab.

2. Press the "More" button ⬚ and then press "Play Memory Movie."

3. Tap the screen and then tap the "More" button ⬤ while the movie plays.

4. Click on "Add to Favorites."

5. Press the "Close" button ✖.

This is how you add someone from your People album to your Memories:

1. Find the album called "People" and tap on it.

2. Click on the person's picture, then click on the "More" button ⬤.

3. Press **"Create Photo Memory."**

Save your favorite memories

1. Click on the "For You" tab and pick a date.

2. Press "Add to Favorites" after pressing "More ⬚."

On the "For You" tab, tap "See All" next to "Memories," and then tap "Favorites." This will show you your favorite memories. Just tap the Favorite button ♥ again if you change your mind about saving a memory.

Share your favorite memories

1. When you play a Memory movie, you can tap the screen to see the editing and sharing choices.

2. Pick how you want to share after pressing the Share button .

The song is shared when you share a memory. You will be asked to pick a song that can be shared with the memory if a certain song can't be shared.

Edit your memories

You can change some things about your Memories to make them even more unique. What you can do with a memory is change its title and add or remove photos. You can also change its length based on the number of photos it has.

Change the title

1. Press the "More" button in the memory area.

2. Press Edit Title, then click "Save."

Add and remove photos within a memory

1. Play a memory, then tap the screen.
2. Press the "More" button ⬤, and then press "Manage Photos."
3. Check photos to add them or deselect the photos you want to remove.
4. Press **"Done."**

To make a photo the key photo for a memory

1. Press the "Pause" button ❚❚ after playing the video.
2. Press the "More" button ⬤ and then press "Make Key Photo."

To hide a specific photo from a memory

1. Press the "Pause" button ❚❚ after playing the video.
2. Press "More" ⬤ and then "Hide From Memory."

Change the length of a memory

1. Once you're done, tap the screen.

2. Press "More ," then "Short," "Medium," or "Long."

Your phone may only show you Short and Medium length choices if it has a lot of photos stored.

Apple Photo Album
Add a picture to a shared album
Step 1: Open the Photos app and pick the Photos tab from the list at the bottom. What you can choose is Years, Months, Days, or All Photos, based on your taste.

Step 2: Tap on a picture or video to add it to an Album. Press Select and then select to add more than one file.

Step 3: Click the Share button in the bottom left corner of the window once you've made your choice.

Step 4: From the drop-down menu, choose "Add to Album" or "Add to Shared Album."

Step 5: Make a new album or select an existing one to which the photo will be added.

How to Create a New Album on the iPhone Photos App

Step 1: Open the Photos app on your iPhone 15 models and select Albums from the list at the bottom.

Step 2: Tap the "+" sign in the upper left corner of the window.

Step 3: Choose either "New Album" or "New Shared Album".

Step 4: Save the album and give it a name you like.

Step 5: Pick out the photos you want to add to the new album, then click **"Done."**

Delete Photos and Videos from Existing Albums

Step 1: Open the Photos app and go to the Albums tab.

Step 2: Pick out the video or picture you want to get rid of and tap on it. If you wish to delete several files, click Select and select the files you want to remove.

Step 3: Press the **Delete** button in the bottom right part of the screen.

Step 4: Tap Remove from Album to get rid of the file from the album.

Note that this will only remove the picture from the album, not the file from the camera roll.

Remove an album from my iPhone

There is an easy way to delete an album on your iPhone. To get started, just follow these steps:

1. In the Photos app, go to the bottom and tap Albums.
2. Next to My Albums, tap See All at the top.
3. Click on Edit.
4. Tap the red "-" sign next to the album(s) you want to get rid of.
5. When you're done, press "Done."

How can I remove the Favorites album from my computer?

It's too bad that you can't get rid of the Favorites album from your computer. Like the Recents album, Favorites is one of the albums that the Photos app makes by default, and you can't move, change, or delete it.

Here's what you need to do to get rid of the pictures:

1. Go to Photos to open the album.
2. From the drop-down menu, choose **Select > Select All.**
3. Tap the trash can icon in the bottom right spot.

After following the steps in the last part, you can now get rid of the album.

Step 3: On iPhone, place pictures in a secret album (optional)

You can hide photos in your Camera Roll if you want to keep private or sensitive photos but don't want them to be seen by everyone. To keep all of your hidden pictures safe, you could also make a secret book.

How to make a hidden album

Your Hidden album will show up if you've chosen to hide a picture. This is how you would hide a picture:

1. Find the picture you want to hide in the Photos app and touch it.

2. Tap the Share button in the bottom right spot.

3. From the drop-down menu, scroll down and pick "Hide."

How to update the Hidden Album with fresh pictures

If you hide one picture, a Hidden album will appear, and you can add more photos to it. Here's what you need to do to add new photos to your album.

1. Tap the **Library tab** at the bottom of the Photos app.

2. Touch the picture you want to upload for each one.

3. Touch the Share button in the bottom right spot, then touch Hide.

Hidden Album

1. Open the app called Settings.

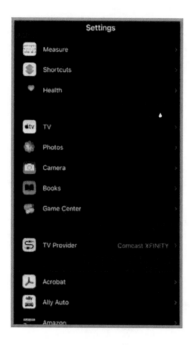

2. Pick out Photos.

3. From the drop-down box, choose **"Enable Hidden."**

To see all of your secret photos, go back to the Photos app and select **Albums > Hidden.**

Step 4: Put your photos in the right folders.

If you have a lot of photos in your library, scrolling through your Camera Roll might not be the best way to find the ones you want. When you put your pictures in albums, it's much easier to find the ones you want.

How to organize pictures in your album

It's very simple to take pictures with your iPhone. But putting those pictures together isn't nearly as fun. It might not be as hard as it looks, thank goodness. Your picture collection doesn't have to be hard to organize just because it's big.

Step 1: Clean up your iPhone shots before you organize them.

Getting rid of the things you don't want will save you a lot of time when you're going through your picture library. There is good news: Gemini pictures let you scan your pictures and quickly get rid of the extra ones. The program looks for copies, screenshots, notes, fuzzy pictures, and even pictures that look a lot alike.

Get Gemini Photos from the App Store, open it on your iPhone, and follow these steps to clean up your library.

Identical-looking images

1. Click on Similar. Your pictures will be put in order by date or event.
2. Pick out a group. This sign will pick the best pictures for you.
3. Pick the sets you want and press "Move to Trash" for each one.
4. Once you're done, press Empty Trash and then tap Delete to confirm.

Duplicates

1. You can choose Duplicates from the choice that drops down. Gemini Photographs can find all of the similar photos on your iPhone.
2. Tap on each group of copies to look at them again.
3. Once you're done with all of them, go to the bottom of the screen and click Delete Duplicates.

4. Tap Delete to make sure.

Videos
1. Pick Videos. The videos in your collection will be shown in Gemini Photos, along with how much space they take up.
2. You can swipe up to keep a video and down to delete it.
3. Tap Empty Trash at the bottom of the screen.

Screenshots
1. From the window that drops down, choose Screenshots. Gemini Photos will pick out all of your screenshot shots for you.
2. If you want to keep some of them, uncheck the boxes next to them.
3. At the bottom of the screen, tap Delete. Then, tap Delete All.

Notes
1. Click on "Notes." The program will look through your pictures and put together any pictures of whiteboards or notebooks that it finds.
2. Tap on the pictures you want to get rid of.

3. Press Delete All at the bottom when you're done.

Blurred

1. If you click on Blurred, you can see all of the blurry pictures that Gemini Photos found.
2. Get rid of the pictures you don't want to keep.
3. Press Delete to confirm, then press Delete again.

Other

1. Some pictures don't belong in any of the other groups. Tap "Other" to see them. Your pictures will be put in order by when they were taken.
2. Tap on a month to choose it.
3. To save a picture, swipe up on it. To delete it, swipe down.
4. Once you're done with all of these files, click "Empty Trash" at the bottom of the screen.
5. Close the library and open the pictures app. To get rid of the pictures on your iPhone, go to **Albums > Recently Deleted > Select > Delete All.** If you don't, they will stay on your computer for 30 days and take up space.

Step 2: Delete any iPhone picture albums that you no longer need.

You might find old albums you don't want in the Album tab of the Photos app on your iPhone. You might also see albums made by other apps, like WhatsApp or Snapchat. It's better to delete songs that you're not using so that they don't take up space on your phone and make it hard to find the ones you need.

What are the steps for adding pictures to the Favorites album?

To add a picture to your Favorites list, do the following:

1. Find the picture you want to share in the Photos app.
2. To fill it in, tap the heart icon at the bottom of the screen.

How to organize your photos into albums based on where they were taken

On top of that, the Photos app makes it easy to make an album based on where the picture was taken. Do these things:

1. Tap the **Search tab** at the bottom of the Photos app.
2. In the Search box, type a location.
3. Tap **See All > Select** to see the list of choices and then tap one.
4. Pick out all the pictures you want to add to a book with your finger.
5. From the drop-down menu, choose **Share, Add to Album, and then New Album.**
6. Name your album and save it.

If you want to add more pictures to an album based on where they were taken, go back to steps 1 through 5 and touch the album instead of clicking "New Album."

How to organize your iPhone photos into themed albums

Using the search function in Photos, you can put all of your beach trip photos or pictures of cool old cars in order. Click on the picture to see how to make an album based on its theme:

1. In the Photos app, go to the bottom and tap Search.
2. Type a theme, like "beach," into the Search box.

3. Tap **See All** > **Select** to see the list of choices and then tap one.

4. Pick out all the pictures you want to put in an album.

5. Go to the bottom of the **screen** > **Add to Album** > **New Album** and tap the Share button.

6. Name the album and save it.

How to make people-categorize picture albums

One of the coolest things about the Photos app is that it can recognize your face. It looks at your pictures and tries to figure out who everyone is in them. So, here's what you'd do if you wanted to make a record about a certain person:

1. Tap the **Albums tab** at the bottom of the Photos app.

2. Under "People & Places," scroll down and tap "People." Pick someone after that.

3. By hitting Select, you can choose all of the photos you want to add to your album.

4. Select the **Share option** > **Add to Collection** > **A new album**.

5. Name your album and save it.

If all you want to do is tag someone that photos have already found in your photos, do the following:

1. Go to the Photos tab and choose Albums.
2. From the People & Places menu, choose People & Places.
3. Pick out the person you want to tag.
4. At the top, tap "Add Name."
5. Type the person's name and then press "Next."
6. Photos will give you more pictures of that person. Once you've chosen all the right things, tap "Done."

How to rename an iPhone picture album

You can change the names of your songs at any time by following these steps:

1. Pick up the Photos app and tap on the Albums tab.
2. Tap on the album you want to change the name to open it.
3. You can choose "Rename Album" from the ellipses button.
4. After you type in the new name for the album, click Save.

Other Tips For the Camera

How to set white balance

Because your photos might not show colors the way they should, white balance helps you get better pictures of them. It makes the white part of the picture look white, which lets the other colors in the picture show up correctly.

The white balance setting on the camera app is different from the one on the VSCO camera. It has an auto-white balance setting, but you can't change the color temperature.

It also comes with several presets that can be used to quickly change the white balance to fit different lighting conditions. You can choose from Shade, Cloudy, Flash, Daylight, Fluorescent, Incandescent, Sunrise/Sunset, and Candlelight.

The idea is that all you have to do is pick the setting that works best with the lighting you have, and any color cast that light might cause should go away.

1. Make sure the Camera+ app is in camera mode. If you can't see the viewfinder, tap the camera button on the screen.

2. To change the white balance, click the WB symbol in the settings menu, which is between the lens and the black bar that holds the shutter button. A list of White Balance settings will show up below the screen.

3. If you swipe horizontally to the left or right, you can see more choices. If you want to see how each setting changes the colors in the camera, click on them.

4. As you look through the presets, you'll find that the color temperature changes a lot. ***Note: Look closely at the white parts of the picture because that's where you'll see the color the most.***

5. You should pick a white balance setting that works well with the light you have used. If you're taking pictures outside on a cloudy day, click on the white balance settings.

6. You should take the time to look at these choices. There are times when the presets work better than the Auto choice at getting rid of color casts.

7. To hide the list of white balance settings while you're shooting, just click on the white balance icon above the list of presets.

8. You can always click on the white balance icon to see the current white balance setting. To go back to the Auto white balance, click on Auto in the list of presets.

9. Once you're happy with the colors and white balance in the viewfinder, press the shutter button to take a shot.

How to correct camera lens flaws

There are different problems that camera lenses can have at different focal lengths, f-stops, and focus distances. You can fix these problems by going to the Lens Corrections tab in the Camera Raw dialog box.

How to automatically fix camera lens defects in your iPhone 15 models

1. On the Lens Corrections menu, find the Profile tab and click on Enable Lens Profile Corrections.

2. If Camera Raw can't find a suitable profile on its own, choose a Make, Model, and Profile.

3. You can change how much adjustment the profile does by moving the Amount sliders. **Distortion:** When you set the distortion to 100, all of the distortion in the picture is fixed. Values above 100 fix distortions better than values below 100; values below 100 fix distortions less well.

4. If you want to use the changes you made to the basic profile, click Setup and then **Save New Lens Profile.**

Manually correcting camera lens defects

1. In the Camera Raw dialog box, go to the Lens Corrections menu and select the Manual tab.

2. Here are the changes you should make to the Distortion box:

   - **Amount:** Move the tool to the right to fix barrel distortion and straighten lines that move away from the middle.

   - To fix pincushion distortion and make lines that move toward the middle straight, move the tool to the left.

3. Under "Defringe," make any of the following changes:
   - Get rid of the purple and green edges around the whole image using the Eyedropper tool:
   - To start picking out the right colors, zoom in on the edges.
   - To get the Eyedropper tool, hold down Command or Control while you tap on the picture.
   - Pick the purple or green fringe color from the drop-down choice.
   - To get rid of the purple and green edges around the image, use the Defringe slider settings.
   - Purple Amount and Green Amount show the amount of defining that was done on the chosen Purple color or Green color. As the number goes up, more color defining is done.
   - **Purple Hue/Green color:** The purple hue/green color doesn't fit in with the chosen hue range. Move either endpoint control to broaden or narrow the color range that is affected. Change the endpoint settings

to change the color range. It takes ten units to get from one endpoint to the other.

4. **Make the following changes to Vignette:**

- To make the edges of the picture lighter, move the Amount tool to the right where there are positive numbers. Move the Amount slider to the left until it shows a negative number. This will make the edges of the picture darker.

- **Midpoint:** To make changes to the Amount in a larger area that isn't in the corners, move the midpoint slider to the left, where the numbers are lower. If you want to stop the change in an area closer to the corners, move the slider to the right, where the numbers are higher.

How to create a preset for a user

Making a preset in Lightroom Mobile is a quick and easy way to give multiple photos the same effect or change. How to do it:

Step 1: Figure out what you want to change about your picture and click the three dots in the top right corner of the screen.

Step 1: Choose Create Preset from the menu that drops down.

Step 3: Give the preset a name and choose which factors to include. Click the check to save the preset.

Step 4: Pick out the picture you want to use the preset on and click the preset button.

Step 5: Press the picture to see what the setting will look like, then tap the checkbox to use it.

How to adjust the tonal scale of a photo

Tonal scale is a property of an image that shows how much contrast or detail there is in the picture. There are a certain amount of pixels in the picture, which range from darkest to lightest.

1. Take a look at Windows and then select the histogram tab from the Navigator panel group

to see it. Then, pick **Expanded View** from the palette menu.

2. To get to the levels dialog box, pick out a picture, go to Adjustments, and then click on Levels.

3. Check the box next to Preview, and then change the settings in the dialog box so that you can see the picture window and the Histogram panel.

4. The darkest colors have started to show up on the right side of the histogram, where the left triangle is now.

5. The lightest colors seem to have started on the left side of the histogram, where the right triangle should be moved.

6. Move the center triangle a little to the left to make the mid-tones lighter.

7. Once you are happy with your work, hit the **OK button** to make the changes and then save the picture.

Made in United States
North Haven, CT
19 November 2023

44278670R00085